AMISH DOLL QUILTS,
Dolls, and Other
Playthings

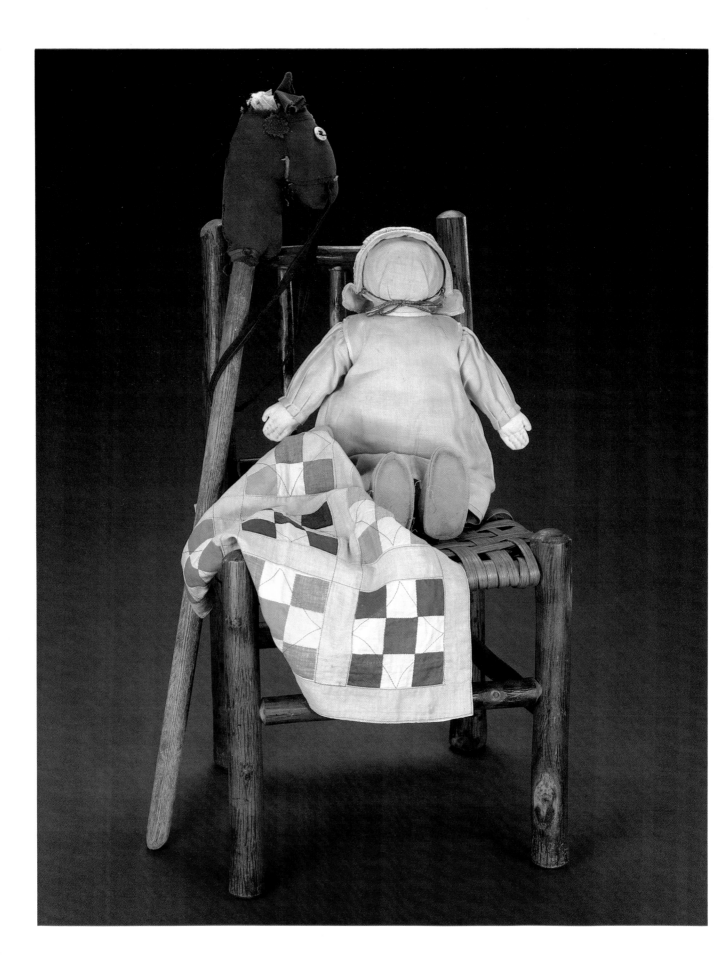

AMISH DOLL QUILTS,
Dolls, and Other
Playthings

Rachel and Kenneth Pellman

Good Books

Intercourse, Pennsylvania 17534

Acknowledgments

We wish to give special thanks to the many, many local and distant Amish neighbors who assisted us in our primary research about their quilts, dolls, and toys. Numerous other folks have contributed their knowledge and memories. Our thanks to each of them. Thanks also to I Love Country and The Old Country Store, both of Intercourse, Pennsylvania, and to Diana Leone, for providing props used in photographs included in this volume. And finally we are delighted and gratified by the cooperation of all the people who generously permitted us to exhibit their treasures on the following pages.

Design by Craig N. Heisey
Cover photo: Jonathan Charles
All photos throughout the book were taken by Jonathan Charles.

All specifications of the artifacts displayed in this book were given to the authors by the current owners.

Amish Doll Quilts, Dolls, and Other Playthings

Copyright © 1986 by Good Books, Intercourse, PA 17534
International Standard Book Number: 0-934672-35-0
Library of Congress Catalog Card Number: 86-81060

Contents

Amish Doll Quilts   7

Amish Dolls   43

Amish Children's Toys and Playthings   79

Who Are These People?   94

Readings and Sources   95

Index   96

Amish Doll Quilts

For years quilts have provided Amish women with a compatible combination of work and pleasure. In fact, it is often difficult to distinguish between a quilt made of necessity and one made for the creative diversion it allowed its maker. Doll quilts are no exception. One difference, however, is that while sometimes made by adults, these little bed and cradle covers were frequently wrought by the hands of young children.

Sewing skills are developed and encouraged in Amish girls at an early age. One Amish woman stated that she still treasures a piece of carefully worked embroidery she completed at age six. Doll quilts were also projects commonly given to girls learning and practicing needlework. Making a doll quilt could wholesomely occupy a little girl for hours. Not only was she playing mother to her baby, she was also practicing domestic skills expected of women within the Amish community. She was playing while learning a valuable lesson.

These lessons seem to have paid off—Amish women continue to be known for their fine craftsmanship in the arena of domestic work. Amish cooking and Amish quilts are widely recognized as some of the best. It is tempting to believe that in setting sharp and clear parameters for its members, the Amish community stifles creativity and appreciation of beauty. Instead, it seems the Amish are more alert to the simple beauty of nature, and that creativity bursts forth in bountiful

meals, well-manicured lawns and gardens, and masterful needlework.

Full-Sized Quilts Are Useful and Beautiful

Antique Amish quilts, generally considered to be pre-1940, show excellent craftsmanship in every aspect of their making. Old quilts were constructed using natural fiber fabrics saturated with color. These deep, rich colors combined to make bold, pieced patterns that were then softened with an abundance of feathery quilting stitches.

Amish women continue the tradition of quilting today. However, today's synthetic fabrics and the commercialization of quilting has greatly changed the overall look of quilts. Instead of using all solid color fabrics, many women are buying color-coordinated calicoes for quiltmaking. Polyester batting has replaced the old cotton or blanket-type linings. Quilting is much less abundant and fine. It is simply not practical to over-invest oneself in a quilt being made to sell. Despite all this, quiltmaking continues to be a complement to homemaking duties and Amish women approach quiltmaking with the same attitude as they approach life in general—any job worth doing should be done well.

Antique Amish quilts make a strong, vivid statement about the overall values and disciplines of the Amish communities themselves. Probably the most distinctive features of full-sized Amish quilts are color, pattern, and craftsmanship. Colors tend to be those of Amish clothing—the deep, solid shades that are worn by adults and the bright, merry colors that are reserved for children. Since the majority of Amish clothing is made at home, there is usually an accumulation of leftover fabric scraps that can be utilized in quiltmaking.

Colors and Patterns Distinguish Communities

Antique Amish quilts are usually identified by the area in which they were made—for example, those from the Lancaster County, Pennsylvania, Amish, the Mifflin County, Pennsylvania, Amish, and the midwestern Amish groups of Ohio and Indiana. In general, the Lancaster County quilts are most conservative in both color and pattern. Colors tend to be from only one-half of the color wheel, ranging from darker reds to, and including, darker shades of green. Many of the patterns used require larger units of fabric, such as the Center Diamond and Bars patterns, thus utilizing fewer colors in a quilt top. The Sunshine and Shadow Pattern, on the other hand, is composed of tiny squares in a myriad of colors.

Mifflin County and midwestern quiltmakers seem to have been more adventuresome both in color and pattern. Mifflin County quiltmakers incorporated bright, almost garish hues into their quilts, including the frequent use of bright yellows. Midwestern quilts also display a wider range of colors than do Lancaster quilts. The diversity of pattern choices indicates that those communities had more interaction, and thus traded patterns more frequently, with non-Amish neighbors, since there were fewer Amish in those more scattered areas.

While patterns may have been borrowed from non-Amish quiltmakers, Amish quilts remained distinctive because of the consistent use of only solid-colored fabrics, often pieced against a dark, solid background. The pieced pattern was almost always surrounded by a wide border characteristic of Amish quilts. Lancaster

Embroidered Quilt, 1911. Cotton, 11½ × 12½. Lancaster County, Pennsylvania. Privately owned. (see page 40)

County borders are particularly wide but most Amish quilts have substantial borders.

Covering the interiors of these antique quilts, as well as their borders, is a generous portion of quilting in a variety of graceful, flowing designs and straight lines. Amish women seem to have perfected the art of quilting. Though the quilting thread is often dark and is usually used against a dark background, the tiny, precise stitches mark a graceful and delicate path across the traditionally stark, geometric, pieced designs.

Full-sized Amish quilts can be rather easily categorized according to region and often grouped into pattern and color categories. But such identification becomes more difficult with crib-sized quilts. While many of the same generalizations are true, fewer crib quilts were made and fewer have survived the years, making comparisons harder to draw.

Full-sized quilts, though utilitarian in purpose, were also creative ventures among a people whose creativity is carefully channeled into useful and necessary functions. A quilt, even if preserved in a chest and put on a bed only for display, was a potentially useful bedcover and therefore fit the standard of a wholesome pastime. The energy and time expended in piecing and quilting a quilt were clearly more than needed to provide a cover for warmth. The quilt, for Amish women, was the perfect marriage of beauty and utility.

Crib Quilts Made for Hard Wear

Crib quilts were more utilitarian. Though still distinctly Amish in character, they appear less precise and elaborate in both pattern and quilting designs. There are, of course, those crib quilts that stand as very fine miniatures of full-sized quilts, but they are the exception rather than the rule. These quilts seem to have been made to be used. Knowing the wear and tear that crib quilts were likely to face, their quilters seem to have reserved some of their energy and creativity.

Doll Quilts Made for Practice and Play

Doll quilts were made to be played with and as such did not deserve the attention and care from their creators that large quilts did. When something serves a useful function, such as a full-sized quilt, the excesses of carefully planned fabric usage and elaborate quilting may be justified. Doll quilts, by contrast, were often made from scrap fabrics. They were sometimes machine-quilted, probably in the interest of efficiency. Judging from their uneven lines, many of these quilts appear to have been practice fields for girls learning how to use sewing machines.

Doll beds and cradles were often covered with remains of old blankets. A girl could cut a chunk from a worn-out blanket, hem the edges, and snuggle her baby comfortably. Leftover patches of flannel or other fabric scraps could be hemmed and used as blankets or sheets. Sometimes a pieced top was layered over batting and a backing, and simply knotted rather than quilted.

But an energetic little girl, guided by her mother, grandmother, or older sister, might tackle her own doll quilt. The scarcity of these quilts today is likely a reflection of the value placed on them when they were made. They were practice pieces for beginning sewers, meant to be

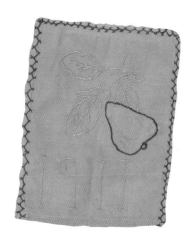

Embroidered Quilt, 1911. Cotton, 11½ × 12½. Lancaster County, Pennsylvania. Privately owned. (see page 40)

played with, worn out, and discarded. The few that have survived often show signs of many hours of wrapping and covering sleeping doll babies.

Doll quilts mirror full-sized quilts and crib quilts in their use of solid color fabrics. Their patterns and the quality of quilting are as individual as the quilts themselves. A few doll quilts were made in such traditional patterns as Center Diamond, Bars, and Sunshine and Shadow. Many, however, are a somewhat haphazard arrangement of geometric shapes and are not beautiful if judged from a strictly aesthetic viewpoint.

There are those exceptional doll quilts that show the same fine quality workmanship as full-sized quilts, but on a miniature scale. However, precise attention to detail in a doll quilt is rare. Because many of these small relics were worked by the hands of an apprentice, one can forgive mismatched corners and long, uneven quilting stitches. They represent the start of a lifetime of sewing. Modeling the work of her mother, a girl could begin with doll quilts and doll clothes, thereby learning the skills of clothing construction and quiltmaking that she would one day use and pass on to her own children.

In Amish communities, male and female roles are clearly defined and respected. A little girl begins domestic chores at an early age and is encouraged to master the tasks that will fall more directly to her as she grows older. Living on a farmstead, often with extended family, she has several role models to emulate. Likewise, little boys are taught the chores of fields and farm. Women, however, are also keenly aware of and often help with the farm operations, and men, many of them working full-time at home, are heavily involved in the upbringing of their children. Despite that, girls soon learn, through direct action and innuendo, that they will need to acquire domestic skills.

Doll quilts represent hours of fun. They also symbolically stand for the creative and protective role girls are expected to assume as they grow into young women.

Sunshine and Shadow, *c. 1940.*
Cotton, 16¼ × 18½. New Wilmington,
Pennsylvania. The People's Place,
Intercourse, Pennsylvania.

Sunshine and Shadow, *c. 1920.*
Cotton, 19 × 18½. Lancaster County,
Pennsylvania. Collection of Nancy
Glazer.

12

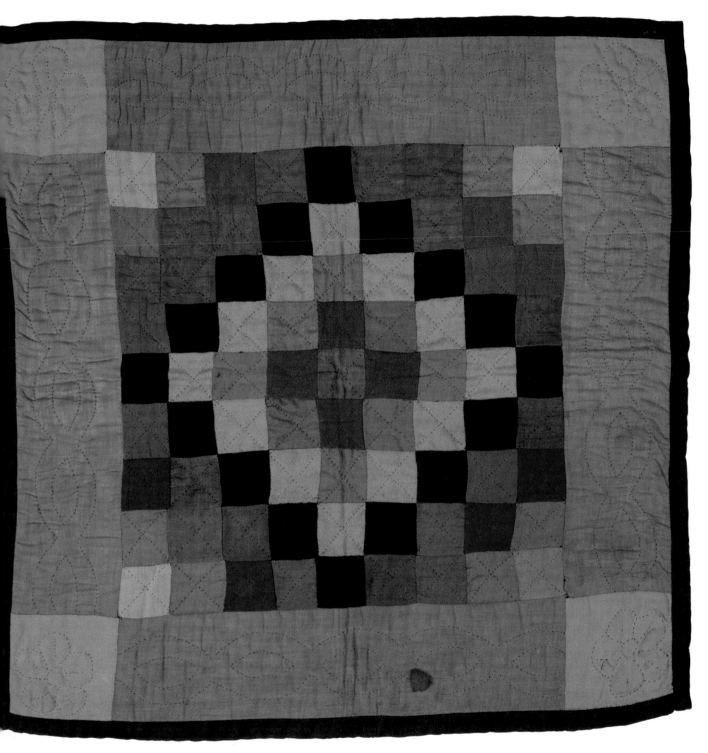

Sunshine and Shadow, *1930s. Wool, wool crepe, and cotton, 23 × 23. Lancaster County, Pennsylvania. Collection of Eve and David Wheatcroft.*

Trip Around the World, c. 1940. Cotton, 19½ × 24. New Wilmington, Pennsylvania. The People's Place, Intercourse, Pennsylvania.

Sunshine and Shadow, c. 1940. Cotton, 11½ × 15. Ohio. The People's Place, Intercourse, Pennsylvania.

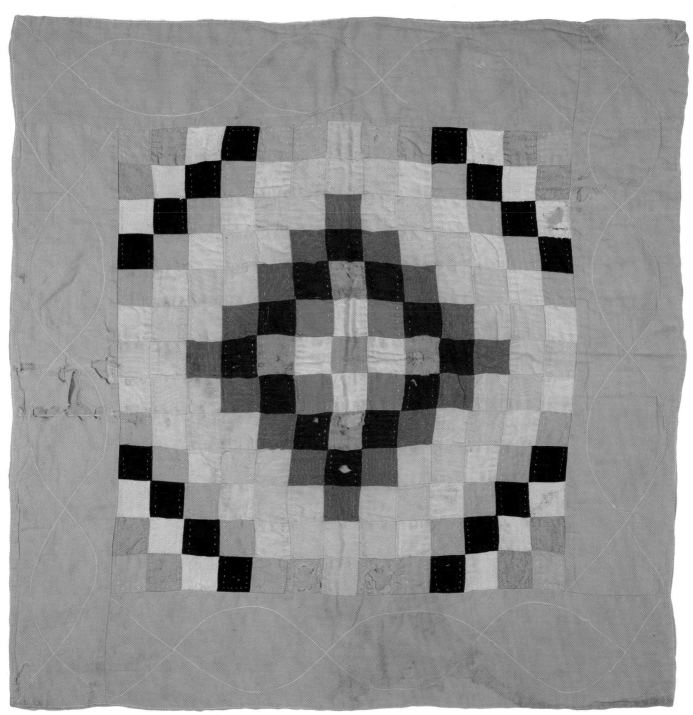

Sunshine and Shadow, *1930–1940. Cotton, 19½ × 19½. Lancaster County, Pennsylvania. The People's Place, Intercourse, Pennsylvania.*

One Patch, *1900–1925. Wool, 11 × 13. Lancaster County, Pennsylvania. Ron and Marilyn Kowaleski.*

One Patch, *1915. Cotton, 21 × 14. Nappanee, Indiana. Collection of Evelyn Gleason.*

One Patch, *1910–20. Wool, 16¼ × 16¼. Midwest. Kelter-Malcé Antiques.*

One Patch, *c. 1920. Cotton, 17½ × 17½. Pennsylvania. Kelter-Malcé Antiques.*

One Patch, *1940s. Cotton and rayon, 17½ × 15. Wisconsin. Collection of Eve and David Wheatcroft.*

Checkerboard, *c. 1940. Cotton, 9 × 14. Ohio. The People's Place, Intercourse, Pennsylvania.*

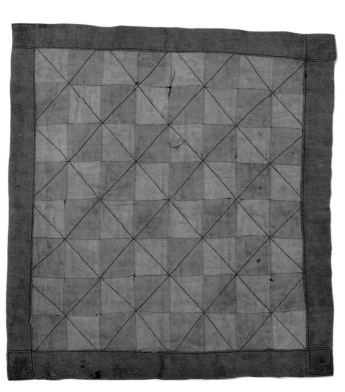

Four-Patch, *c. 1930–1940. Rayon, 4½ × 8. Midwest. Rebecca Haarer, Shipshewana, Indiana.*

Checkerboard, *c. 1910. Wool, 14 × 14. Lancaster County, Pennsylvania. Courtesy of David E. Riehl.*

Checkerboard, *1925–1930. 14½ × 15½. Mifflin County, Pennsylvania. Private collection.*

Four Patch, 1900–1915. Wool, 15 × 18. Lancaster County, Pennsylvania. Ron and Marilyn Kowaleski.

Four Patch, 1905. Cotton and cotton sateen, 19 × 16. Hutchinson, Kansas. Collection of Eve and David Wheatcroft.

One Patch, *1940s. Cotton and cotton sateen, 14½ × 17. Holmes County, Ohio. Collection of Eve and David Wheatcroft.*

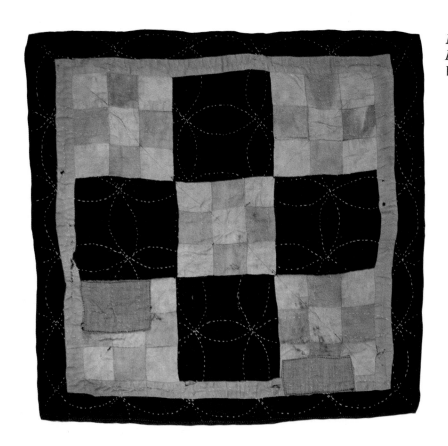

Nine Patch, c. 1920. Cotton, 16 × 16.
Kentucky. Collection of Smith and
Wanda Johnson.

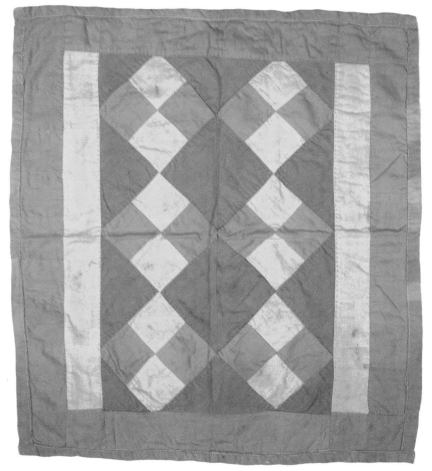

Four Patch, c. 1935. Cotton, 17¾ × 19½.
Clark, Missouri. Collection of Kathryn and
Dan McCauley.

Four Patch, *1921. Cotton, 12½ × 18½. Dover, Delaware. The People's Place, Intercourse, Pennsylvania.*

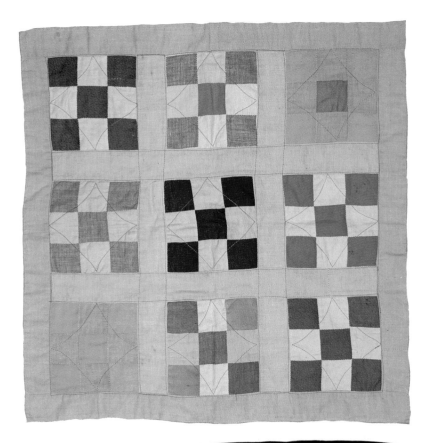

Nine Patch, *c. 1960. Cotton, 16½ × 16½. LaGrange County, Indiana. The People's Place, Intercourse, Pennsylvania.*

Nine Patch Variation, *1930s. Cotton, 18½ × 18½. Mifflin County, Pennsylvania. The People's Place, Intercourse, Pennsylvania.*

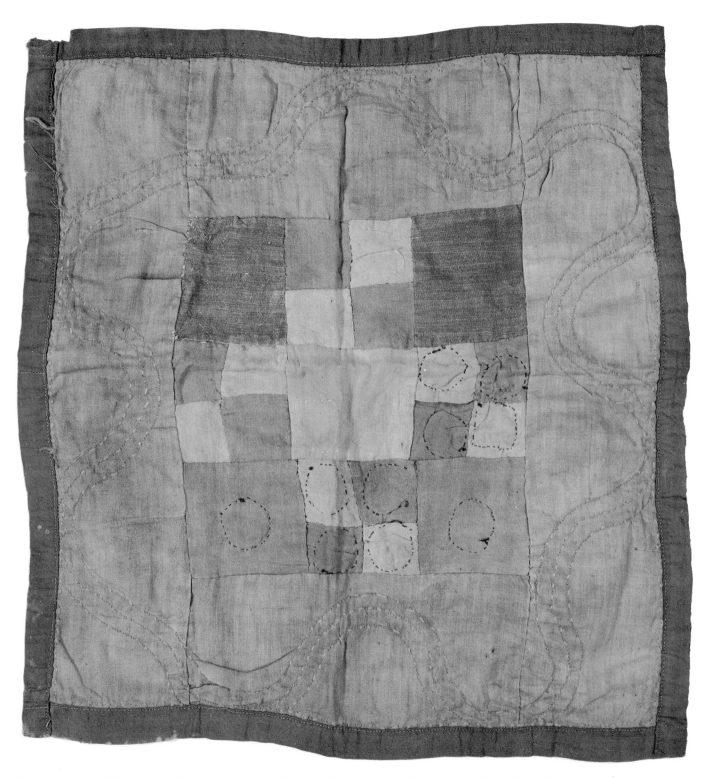

Four Patch, *c. 1928. Cotton, 15 × 14. Lancaster County, Pennsylvania. Dr. and Mrs. Donald M. Herr.*

Nine Patch, *1890. Cotton and wool, 12½ × 15½. Lancaster County, Pennsylvania. Collection of Smith and Wanda Johnson.*

Nine Patch, *c. 1910. Cotton, 12 × 19. Ohio. Joan Fenton and Albie Tabackman/Quilts Unlimited.*

Four Patch, *c. 1940. Cotton, 16½ × 24. Mifflin County, Pennsylvania. The People's Place, Intercourse, Pennsylvania.*

Plain, *c. 1945. Cotton, 19½ × 21½. Conewango, New York. The People's Place, Intercourse, Pennsylvania.*

Open Square, *c. 1930. Wool, 25 × 20½. Pennsylvania. Collection of Nancy Glazer.*

Bars, *c. 1920. Cotton, 20 × 14. Ohio. Collection of Evelyn Gleason.*

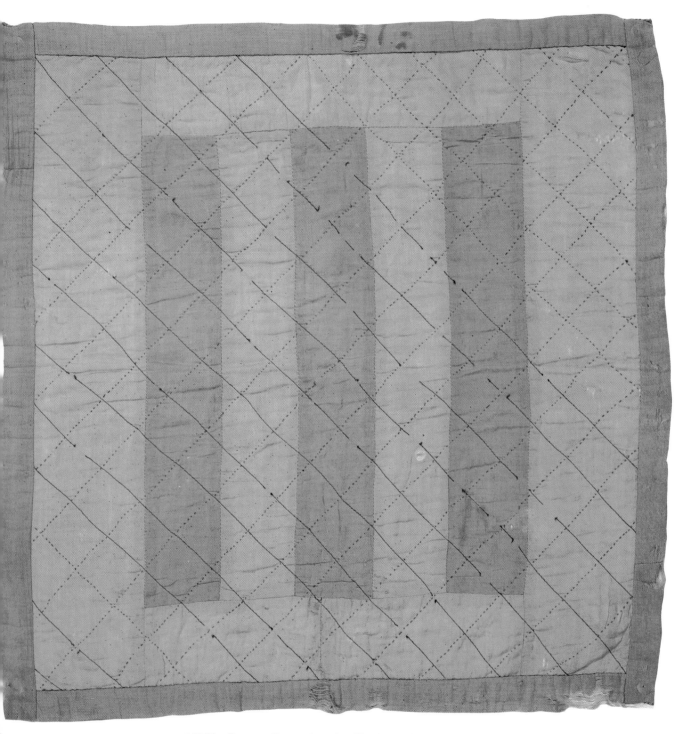

Bars, c. 1920. Wool, 18½ × 18½. *Mifflin County, Pennsylvania. The People's Place, Intercourse, Pennsylvania.*

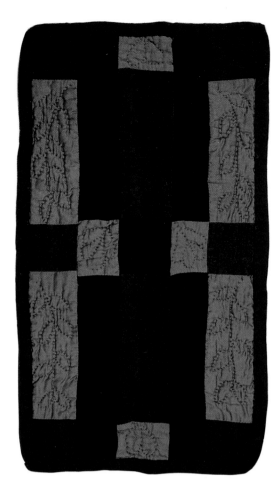

Bars and Blocks, *c. 1920. Cotton, 19½ × 11. Ohio. Collection of Nancy Glazer.*

Chinese Coins, *late 1940s. Cotton, crepe, 14 × 18. Lancaster County, Pennsylvania. Collection of Kathryn and Dan McCauley.*

Concentric Bars. *Cotton, 15 × 19½. Ohio. The People's Place, Intercourse, Pennsylvania.*

Chinese Coins, *c. 1950. Cotton, polyester, 15¾ × 21½. Holmes County, Ohio. The People's Place, Intercourse, Pennsylvania.*

Streak of Lightning, c. 1890. Wool, 16¾ × 14. Lancaster County, Pennsylvania. Collection of Nancy Glazer.

Log Cabin, c. 1935. Cotton, wool, 16 × 16. St. Mary's County, Maryland. Collection of Kathryn and Dan McCauley.

34

Streak of Lightning, *c. 1890. Cotton, 26½ × 19½. Indiana. Collection of Evelyn Gleason.*

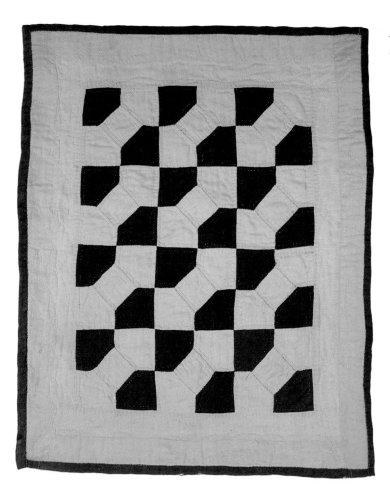

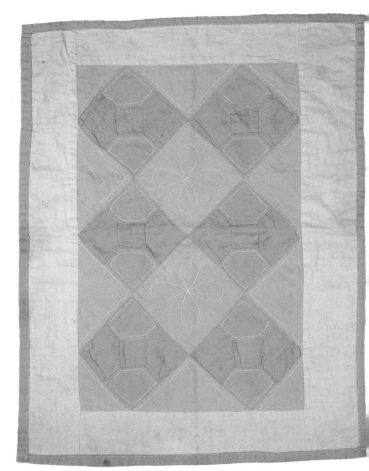

Bow Ties. c. 1910–1920. Cotton, 18½ × 28¾. Ohio. Laura Fisher/Antique Quilts and Americana, New York City.

Bow Ties, 1935–45. Cotton, 17 × 21. Dover, Delaware. Collection of Kathryn and Dan McCauley.

Bow Ties, *1915. Cotton. 13 × 16. Haven, Kansas. Collection of Kathryn and Dan McCauley.*

Tumbling Star, *1955. Cotton, 18¾ × 19¼. Somerset County, Pennsylvania. The People's Place, Intercourse, Pennsylvania.*

Flag Stars, *1950s. Cotton, 13 × 15. Wilton, Wisconsin. The People's Place, Intercourse, Pennsylvania.*

Job's Tears, *c. 1925. Cotton, 12 × 20. Indiana. Collection of Donna and Jonathan Speigel.*

Stars, c. 1940s. Cotton, 12½ × 16. Mifflin County, Pennsylvania. Collection of Eve and David Wheatcroft.

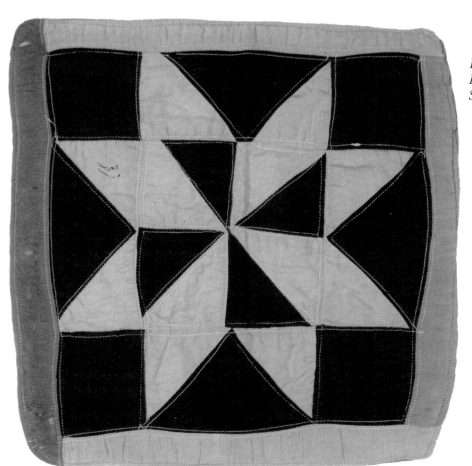

Pinwheel Star, *c. 1920. Cotton, 10 × 10. Indiana. Rebecca Haarer and Joseph M.B Sarah.*

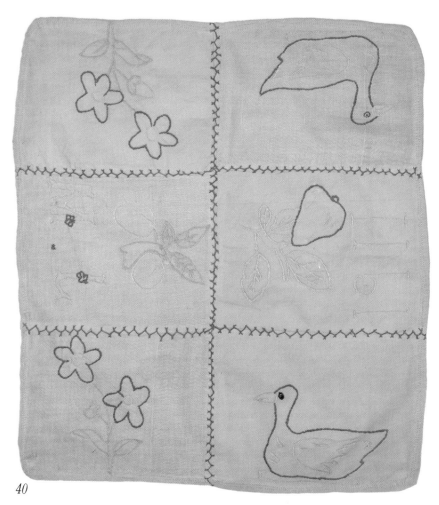

Embroidered Quilt, *1911. Cotton, 11½ × 12½. Lancaster County, Pennsylvania. Privately owned.*

40

Shoo-fly, *c. 1910–1920. Cotton, 15 × 17. Indiana. Rebecca Haarer, Shipshewana, Indiana.*

Amish Dolls

One of the most distinctive features of antique Amish dolls is that the majority of them lack faces. Although there are no written rules mandating this practice, it seems to be associated with the biblical caution in Deuteronomy: "Thou shalt not make unto thee any graven image, or any likeness of anything that is in heaven above, or that is in the earth beneath, or that is in the water under the earth."

In 1865, during a meeting of ministers from Amish communities throughout the U.S., a statement was made banning the use of photography. "Decided, not to allow gaily-colored, checked, striped, or flowered clothing made according to the fashions of the world," it read, "or parting the hair of man or woman after the worldly styles, or carrying hidden on one's person photographic pictures of human likenesses or hanging them on the wall to look at in our houses." One Amish bishop recalled that at that same time his grandfather spoke against having hair and faces on dolls. These two features made them too similar to the likeness of a person and were therefore discouraged.

The fact that dolls were without faces did not seem to pose a problem for the children who played with them. It was simply accepted as the way Amish dolls were. One woman, remembering fondly her days of playing with dolls, explained, "Our homemade dolls had no faces. The clothes were made like ours at that time, mostly cottons, even out of feed sacks. We got our chicken feed in cloth sacks in white, green, blue, and pink. We used the white to make sheets, pillow cases, and underclothes." Another recalled, "Our dolls never had faces. They were dressed like little Amish girls and their clothes were sewn on so we would not remove them." In simple acceptance of the faceless element, one woman stated, "Most rag dolls did not have faces, they were just stuffed with rags and by being dressed you could see which was the face and which was the back of the head."

Another said, "We were not allowed to have store-bought dolls so we just never thought about putting faces on our dolls. I don't think my friends' dolls had any faces, either."

Detail of doll arm with fingered hand. (See page 61)

Dolls Reflect Community's Convictions

While most faceless dolls were constructed with arms and legs of varying detail, some of the most conservative Amish groups drew an even more severe line. Among the Swartzentruber Amish of Ohio, dolls consisted merely of a trunk and head. Arms and legs were considered too realistic. Dresses, however, had sleeves that hung limply by the side. A woman from another conservative group remembered, "Our dolls did not have faces because it was more like the image of a person. I remember there were some mothers that just rolled up a diaper and tied a small scarf on it and put it in a little blanket and used it like a doll."

Faceless dolls seem to have been the norm in most communities but there were always exceptions. One woman recalls, "I had one beautiful doll—a china head, china arms, hands, and feet. It was a real treasure. I always took good care of her. She wore a homemade purple dress and purple cape and a black apron. She was probably given to me with no clothing although I don't remember that part. If she had clothing they were such that my family did not approve of. My mother died when I was six years old and a kindly neighbor lady (not Amish) probably felt sorry for me and gave me the doll. I think a doll with a china head was very unusual at that time [1918]."

Occasionally rag dolls were made with faces, some women remember, "Our dolls had faces. Sometimes they were embroidered and sometimes tiny blue or brown buttons were used for eyes. Our dolls were dressed with the same clothes as the babies, only smaller—plain Amish clothes." Although it seems most children were content to leave them plain, a few antique dolls have crudely drawn facial features probably added on adventuresome days of play.

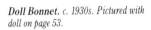

Doll Bonnet. c. 1930s. Pictured with doll on page 53.

Even without eyes, nose, and mouth, a doll's face could be given contours by sewing the head in several sections. This type of doll seems to have been worked from a bought, rather than a homemade, pattern. Contoured-face dolls were also frequently constructed with button joints at shoulders and hips, allowing them more freedom of movement and the ability to sit. Patterns vary a great deal but these dolls were generally more rounded and realistic in appearance.

The most common Amish dolls are somewhat flat with their fronts and backs being very similar. Their arms and legs often end as straight stumps without hands or feet. As a group, Lancaster County Amish dolls are some of the most detailed, often having hands with thumbs and, occasionally, stitched fingers. Many times their feet are tapered to look more natural.

As in other families, Amish mothers, grandmothers, aunts, and older sisters frequently made rag dolls for the little girls. When a girl was named for her grandmother or aunt, she was likely to receive a namesake doll from the honored older woman. Most dolls were made and used within the same family. Occasionally a woman would show outstanding capabilities in doll-making and would make dolls for other families upon request.

Lizzie Lapp Dolls

One very unusual and prolific doll maker was Lizzie Lapp (1860–1932) of Lancaster County, Pennsylvania. Lizzie suffered from a speech impediment that made it difficult for persons to understand her. She spoke mainly in single words and gestures. She never married and filled her days with doll-making.

Her dolls consisted of three basic parts. The head, trunk, and arms were constructed of two identical pieces of fabric sewn together and stuffed with rags. Legs were made as individual units and attached separately so the doll could sit. Hands were also made individually and attached to the arms in a glovelike manner. Lizzie's dolls' hands were almost always of denim and had the distinctive feature of a thumb and four stitched fingers. The hand was only slightly stuffed to give it form. The tapered feet of her dolls were also covered with denim, which extended partway up the leg. She always buried a stick in the rag stuffing between the doll's head and trunk to keep the head upright.

Another feature of Lizzie Lapp dolls was that while the body was made of feed sack or another durable fabric, the faces were white and the backs of the heads were black or some other dark fabric. She achieved this by first making the doll and then making a sheath to fit over the head with its one side white and the other dark. This piece was then hand-stitched in place at the shoulders. The effect was a face on one side (however, without features) and hair on the other. Her dolls wore an Amish-style dress but no cap or bonnet. She sold these dolls from her home, mostly to Amish clientele.

Although most of her dolls were faceless rag dolls, Lizzie would sometimes make china- or metal-head dolls using her same basic pattern but attaching a store-bought head on the cloth body.

Amish families, for the most part, made conscious decisions against the available china, tin, and composition heads, hands, and feet they could have purchased to

make dolls. They also chose against buying ready-made dolls. They preferred, instead, to make dolls for their children in keeping with the values and principles set forth by the church.

Many rag dolls were made in rural areas during the Depression years out of sheer necessity. People simply could not afford to purchase dolls for little girls. But the cloth dolls made by the Amish were not primarily the result of a financial decision. They were made in keeping with the values of simplicity and humility. Extravagance in any area of life was frowned upon. A fussy, frilly doll would not fit into such a lifestyle.

A doll was likely to last a long time. Faces, hands, feet, and other worn or dirty parts could be recovered and the doll was good for another round. It was not unusual for this type of renovation to occur in preparation for Christmas. One woman explained that their dolls always got new, clean faces and often new clothes as part of their cleanup for the holidays. Said another, "It made us feel like we had brand new dolls."

Dolls Reinforce Values

Playing with dolls was also practicing for life. Watching her mother, a little girl could learn what would be expected from her later as an adult. Making clothes for dolls became the first step in learning to make one's own clothes. One woman explained how she and her

sisters cared for their dolls, "We made little bonnets and dresses for them and also shirts and pants for some to have little boys, too. I loved to play with dolls when I had three or four of them in different sizes. We often played church."

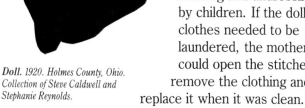

Antique Amish dolls vary greatly in the style and quantity of their clothing. Some wear a simple, solid color dress while others are complete with elaborate petticoats, underwear, full outerwear, Amish head coverings, and bonnets. It is not unusual to find the doll dress stitched on the doll, probably to discourage a lot of dressing and undressing by children. If the doll clothes needed to be laundered, the mother could open the stitches to remove the clothing and replace it when it was clean.

Doll. 1920. Holmes County, Ohio. Collection of Steve Caldwell and Stephanie Reynolds.

The majority of antique Amish dolls are dressed as little girls, though occasionally some are dressed as boys. These boy dolls seldom wear

46

hats. If they have headgear, it is usually a homemade cap or stocking cap similar to what Amish baby boys wear. Though most doll-playing was done by little girls, the incidence of boy dolls suggests that some were made specifically for little boys. One grandmother remarked that even though her grandsons are a bit sheepish about admitting their affection for the boy dolls she made for them, she can see that they like them a great deal.

Change has taken place within the Amish communities. Today it is not unusual to find store-bought dolls in many Amish homes, especially in Lancaster County.

The dolls look Amish only because they are dressed in the traditional Amish garb. Faceless dolls continue to be made and played with in the more conservative settlements, particularly among the midwestern groups. As in former years, articulation of the reasons for faceless dolls is vague. Rather, there seems to be a general acceptance of the church's and faith community's norms so that reasons do not always have to be clearly stated. As one woman said, "I guess in our present day and age a lot of young people lack contentment. If we don't appreciate and are not thankful for what we have, we are discontent."

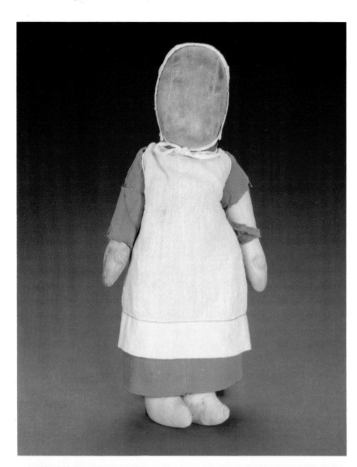

Doll, c. 1940. 14½" high. Indiana. The People's Place, Intercourse, Pennsylvania.

Doll, 1930s. 19" high. Ohio. The People's Place, Intercourse, Pennsylvania.

Doll, *c. 1930. 18" high. Elkhart County, Indiana. Private collection of Diana Leone.*

Doll, c. 1940. 9½" high. Bowling Green, Missouri. The People's Place, Intercourse, Pennsylvania.

Triplet Dolls, c. 1950. 8½" high. Ohio. Joan Fenton and Albie Tabackman/Quilts Unlimited.

Doll, *c. 1930. 18" high. Elkhart County, Indiana. Private collection of Diana Leone.*

Doll, *c. 1925. 13" high. Pennsylvania. Collection of Barbara S. Janos, New York, NY.*

Bottle Doll, 1900. Wool and cotton with glass bottle for body, 4" high. Lancaster County, Pennsylvania. Ron and Marilyn Kowaleski.

Doll, c. 1910. 14" high. Elkhart County, Indiana. Colleen and Louis Picek, Main Street Antiques and Art, West Branch, Iowa.

Doll, c. 1930. 18" high. Elkhart County, Indiana. Private collection of Diana Leone.

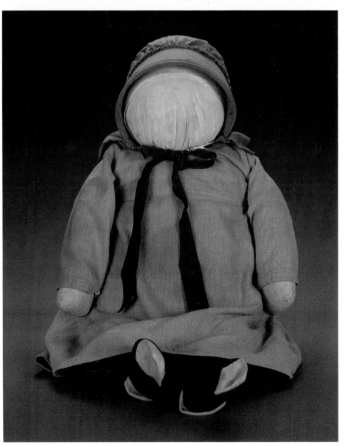

Doll, c. 1930s. 23" high. Kalona, Iowa. Colleen and Louis Picek, Main Street Antiques and Art, West Branch, Iowa.

Doll, *1910–20. Wood composition head with flour sack body, 18" high. Lancaster County, Pennsylvania. Collection of Kathryn and Dan McCauley.*

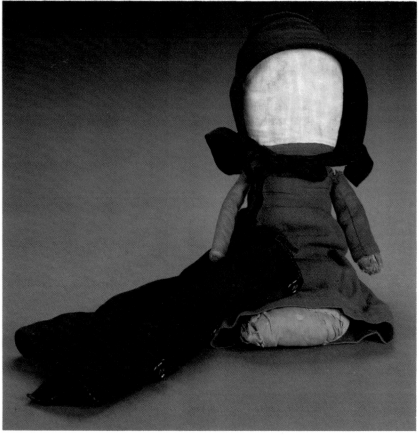

Doll, *c. 1940. 15" high. Ohio. The People's Place Intercourse, Pennsylvania.*

54

Doll, *1940–1950. 19″ high. Ohio. The People's Place, Intercourse, Pennsylvania.*

Doll, c. 1920s. 17" high. Jamesport, Missouri. Colleen and Louis Picek, Main Street Antiques and Art, West Branch, Iowa.

Doll, 1930s. 15½" high. Ohio. The People's Place, Intercourse, Pennsylvania.

Doll, 1930s. Cotton, 7½" high. Amherst, Wisconsin. Collection of Eve and David Wheatcroft.

Doll, *1915–25. Denim, muslin, and cotton with wool yarn hair, 15" high. Lancaster County, Pennsylvania. Collection of Kathryn and Dan McCauley.*

Twin dolls, *1910–1920. 16½" high. Adams County, Indiana. Collection of Kathryn and Dan McCauley.*

Doll, 1900–1910. 7" high. Pennsylvania.
Collection of Barbara S. Janos and Barbara
Ross, New York, NY.

Doll, 1918. Sugar sack head with denim
body. 18½" high. Holmes County, Ohio.
Collection of Kathryn and Dan McCauley.

Doll, *c. 1910. Wool and cotton, 12" high. Lancaster County, Pennsylvania. Courtesy of David E. Riehl.*

Doll, *1880–1910. China head with muslin body, 17½" high. Lancaster County, Pennsylvania. Collection of Kathryn and Dan McCauley.*

Doll, c. 1920. 15" high. Indiana. Antiques in the Country Manner, Shaker Heights, Ohio.

Doll, 1940–1950. 14½" high. Ohio. The People's Place, Intercourse, Pennsylvania.

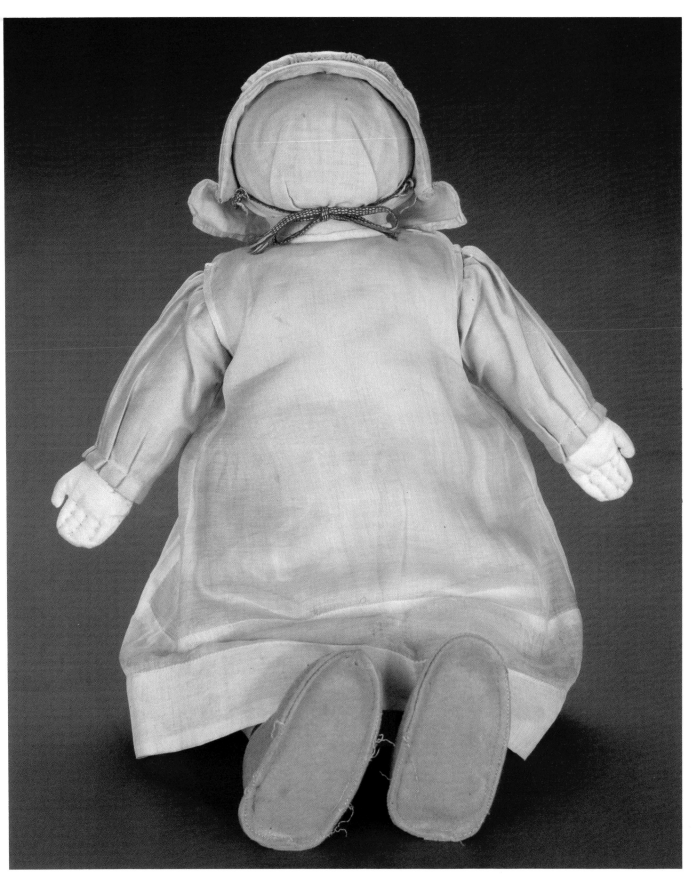

Doll, *c. 1920–1930. 16" high. Elkhart County, Indiana. Rebecca Haarer, Shipshewana, Indiana.*

Doll, c. 1920. Oilcloth head with sock body, 9¼" high. Indiana. Antiques in the Country Manner, Shaker Heights, Ohio. This small doll was taken along to church as entertainment for the baby.

Doll, 1910. 17" high. Lancaster County, Pennsylvania. Collection of Smith and Wanda Johnson.

Doll, *1940s. 13" high. Ohio. The People's Place, Intercourse, Pennsylvania.*

Doll, *c. 1950. 10½" high. Ohio. The People's Place, Intercourse, Pennsylvania. Typical of dolls found among the conservative Swartzentruber Amish, this doll has no arms or legs. The body consists of only a trunk.*

Doll, 1930–1935. 14″ high. Mifflin County, Pennsylvania. Private collection.

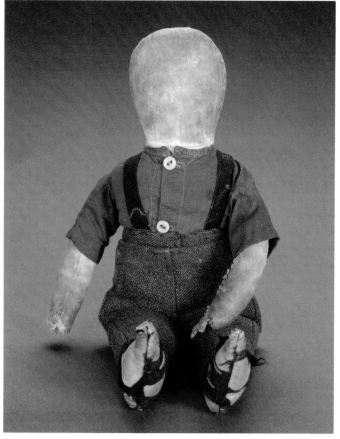

Doll, 1940s. 15½″ high. Iowa. The People's Place, Intercourse, Pennsylvania.

Doll, *c. 1940. 10½" high. Iowa. The People's Place, Intercourse, Pennsylvania.*

Doll, *c. 1900. Cotton, 4" high. Ohio. Collection of Eve and David Wheatcroft.*

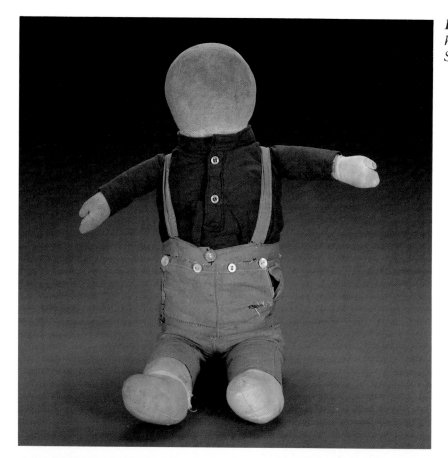

Doll, 1910. Cotton, wool, and corn cobs, 19" high. Holmes County, Ohio. Collection of Stephanie Reynolds and Steve Caldwell.

Doll, 1940s. 13½" high. Indiana. The People's Place, Intercourse, Pennsylvania.

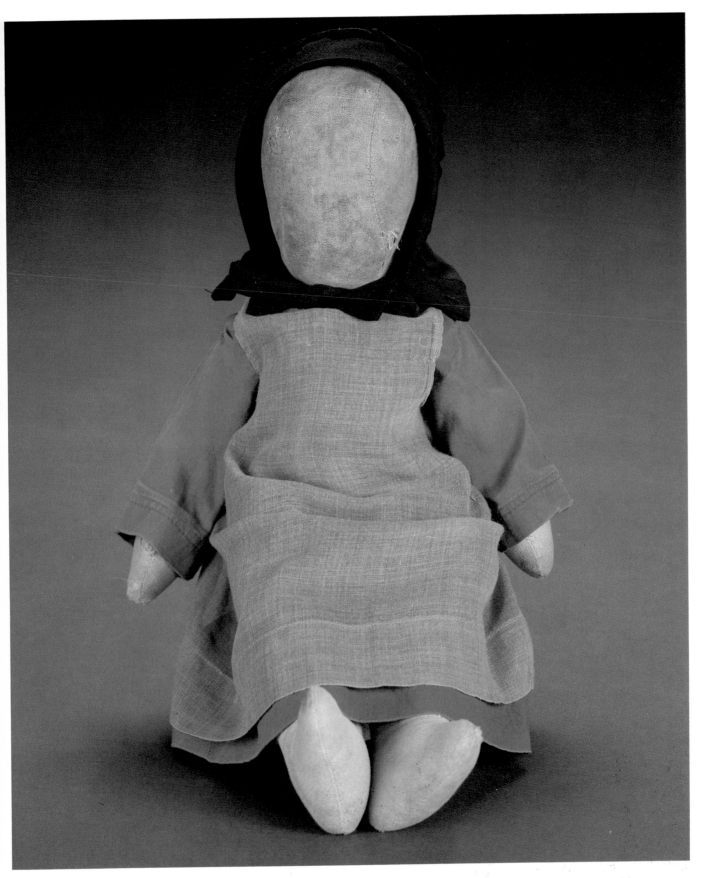

Doll, *c. 1940. 15" high. Ohio. The People's Place, Intercourse, Pennsylvania.*

Doll, *1940–1950. 19" high. Ohio. The People's Place, Intercourse, Pennsylvania.*

Doll, *1940s. 14" high. Ohio. The People's Place, Intercourse, Pennsylvania.*

Doll, *c. 1880. 16½″ high. Lancaster County, Pennsylvania. The People's Place, Intercourse, Pennsylvania.*

Doll, *1930s. 16½" high. Ohio. The People's Place, Intercourse, Pennsylvania.*

Doll, *1925. Tin head with cloth body, 12" high. Lancaster County, Pennsylvania. Collection of Kathryn and Dan McCauley.*

70

Doll, *1930–40. Feed sack body with denim work clothes, 17" high. Lawrence County, Pennsylvania. Collection of Kathryn and Dan McCauley.*

Doll, 1920s. Cotton and wool with rag stuffing, 16" high. Lancaster County, Pennsylvania. Collection of Eve and David Wheatcroft.

Doll, 1910–1915. China head and hands with cloth body. 13" high. Lancaster County, Pennsylvania. Privately owned.
There are exceptions to any generalization. Although this doll is lacking all the markings of a typical Amish doll, it is documented to have been owned and played with by an Old Order Amish family.

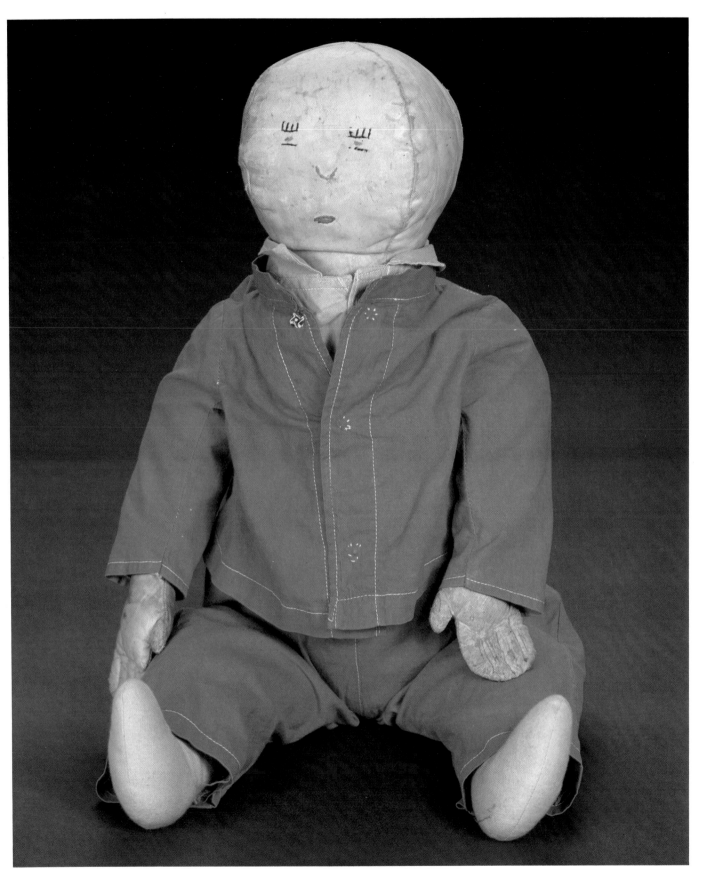

Doll, *1930s. Oilcloth body with rag stuffing, 21" high. Arthur, Illinois. Collection of Eve and David Wheatcroft.*

Doll, c. 1920. Burlap body, 19″ high. Indiana. Antiques in the Country Manner, Shaker Heights, Ohio.

Twin dolls, 1910–1920. 12″ high. Lancaster County, Pennsylvania. Collection of Kathryn and Dan McCauley.

Twin dolls, *1920. Feed sack bodies, denim hands and feet, wool dresses, 14" high. Lancaster County, Pennsylvania. Collection of Kathryn and Dan McCauley. These dolls were made by Lizzie Lapp, an Amish seamstress and dollmaker.*

Doll. 1920s. 16" high. Lancaster County, Pennsylvania. Collection of Smith and Wanda Johnson.

Doll. 1930–1940. Composition head, 18" high. Lancaster County, Pennsylvania. Laura Fisher/Antique Quilts and Americana, New York City.

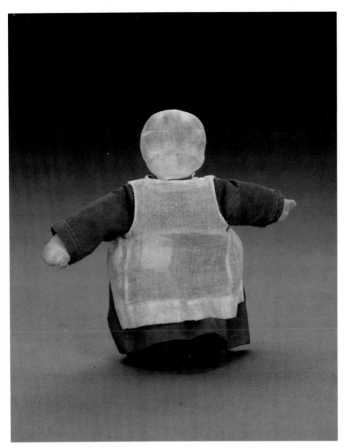

Doll, 1940s. Cotton stuffed with rags, 7" high. Lancaster County, Pennsylvania. Collection of Eve and David Wheatcroft.

Doll, c. 1950. 16½" high. Lancaster County, Pennsylvania. The People's Place, Intercourse, Pennsylvania.

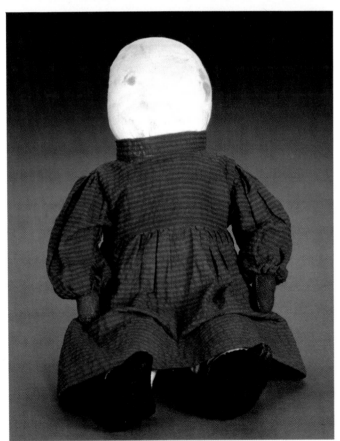

Doll, 1925. Wool and cotton, 20½" high. Holmes County, Ohio. Collection of Stephanie Reynolds and Steve Caldwell.

77

Amish Children's Toys and Playthings

Children and toys go together like lemonade goes with hay-baling. Amish children and their playthings are no different: where one is, the other is bound to be found. And as with other rural folk, especially from the turn of the century through the Great Depression, Amish children have enjoyed playthings other than those found on toy store shelves.

In years gone by, farm families have often had an abundance of chores and a scarcity of store-bought toys. Consequently, in Amish homes, work and play became early partners. Then, as now, children's play often mirrored adult tasks. Among the Amish, children are usually given regular chores at a young age. It is not unusual for a three-year-old to daily gather the eggs from a half-dozen bantam hens. A sense of belonging and being needed comes with specific responsibilities.

The principle that work and play are not rivals, but teammates, is a time-honored practice among these people. An Amish woman remembers that as a child, she had no idle time. "When I was very young, about six of us—three in our family, and three or four of my cousins—had to graze my grandfather's animals: 60 cows (all milked by hand), 40 sheep, and 18 to 20 horses. There were no fences as we have now, and we children had to help as soon as we were five or six years old. We also had the job of carrying water to the men in the fields, our legs getting all scratched up from walking in wheat fields and oat fields after the grain was cut. We

also fixed water containers outside for the threshers to wash their hands. We loved those days!"

The community's religious beliefs are an additional element affecting the number and type of playthings available to Amish children. The church's position against radios, stereos, and television, for example, eliminates a staple found in the play diet of many non-Amish children. Bicycles are also widely disapproved of since they permit easy and speedy access to town and away from home. Scooters, wagons, and kiddie cars are generally permitted, however. In recent years children's tricycles have gained acceptance in some communities.

Amish families are traditionally large. Five to seven children or more per family unit is not unusual. With such an immediate supply of siblings, often very close in age, Amish children seldom lack playmates.

Farms Are Rich in Possibilities

Imagination, creativity, and fun have thrived among these people, both historically and today. Limited cash, church cautions, and a general wariness of excesses have led to abundant ingenuity and invention.

One family recalls that they were lucky enough to have a big playhouse. "It wasn't fancy, probably 10 feet by 12 feet, and was used as a smokehouse in the winter to smoke the home-butchered hams. But we moved our playthings out there in the summer. We had a table, chairs, little benches and so on, some dishes, pans, and big imaginations." A simple stick can, on a moment's notice, become a stick horse. Brooms make an easy transition from sweeping utensil to horse. Unfortunately, mothers sometimes have difficulty corralling their needed brooms! Empty grocery boxes and cans are perfect for playing house, peddler, and storekeeper. A box can become a barn, spools a fence, round rings a water tank, and gourds and corn cobs cows and horses.

Limitations foster creativity. One older Amish person instructed, "Pick a hollyhock flower that is completely open, leaving one-half inch of stem on it. Now pick a bud that you can't see the color of yet. Peel off all the green. You will find holes at the bottom. Insert the stem of the flower in one hole and it will look like a face on the one side (don't leave any stem on the bud). Now it is ready to float. Put the flower face down in the water. It will look like a dress. As children we used to float them on the stock watering tank."

Stilts are playthings frequently found on Amish farms. There is always enough wood around to make a pair without any expense. One man recalls, "I made my stilts out of 1 × 2 wood with a block nailed on the flat side about 16 to 18 inches off the ground." Often fathers and sons or brothers and sisters would help each other make a pair of stilts. One woman remembers, "My brothers made just small stilts for us girls. But they used to have such big ones that they would have to climb on the porch roof to get on them."

Water has provided much opportunity for play for Amish children. It is usually plentiful on an Amish farm, from watering troughs for animals and pump troughs near the house to streams meandering lazily through the pastureland and farm ponds that are a reservoir in case of fire. Aside from wading, swimming, and ice skating, these water sources offer hours of enjoyment for children.

There are polliwogs to catch and watch until they turn to frogs. There are objects to be floated downstream. One woman reminisces, "Paper boats were made easily of newspaper or any other paper big enough. We often just let them float. Sometimes we fastened on paper

Corncob cat, c. 1940. Kalona, Iowa. Privately owned.

sails. These actually worked, blown by the wind. And often before sailing the folded papers, we used them as hats. Usually we each had one on our heads, down by the creek where no one saw us!"

Overgrown cucumbers were also launched in the farm pond flotilla. "These large cucumbers were carefully hollowed out and most of the pulp removed. The skin was not to be punctured below or the boat would sink. Each of us started our boats together. The one going the longest distance before sinking was the winner."

Another who spent hours along the stream remembers, "We used a stick, some heavy twine I got off feed bags, and a crooked pin to go fishing. And believe it or not, I did catch a few little fish that way. These fish were always very small so we usually tossed them back or put them in the water trough in the barn where they didn't live too long. Usually the cats ended up getting them for a treat."

Dirt and water together have universal appeal for play. Add lime, another handy resource on the farm, and the fun multiplies. One woman tells of mud cakes frosted with the lime that her dad used to paint the barn floors. "The lime was mixed with water, just enough to make it thick enough to cover the mud cake. One time we made a mud cake and shaped it like a layer cake and frosted it with lime. I put it on the dinner table and Mother played along with us. We even passed the cake at the dinner table to our father. We had lots of fun trying to fool him!"

Togetherness Is a Strong Value

Old Order Amish families neither own nor drive cars. The result: they have more time at home together. Many families tell stories about working and playing together.

Fathers and brothers have often made doll beds and furniture for the girls. Mothers design and construct dolls and stuffed animals for the children. Fabric scraps from other sewing projects are abundant and serve as stuffing material. Some of the more conservative Amish groups, who are cautious about making realistic models of humans in doll form, do permit toy animals. An animal, complete with eyes, nose, and mouth, is not seen as a challenge to the reference in the Ten Commandments against making "graven images," as a

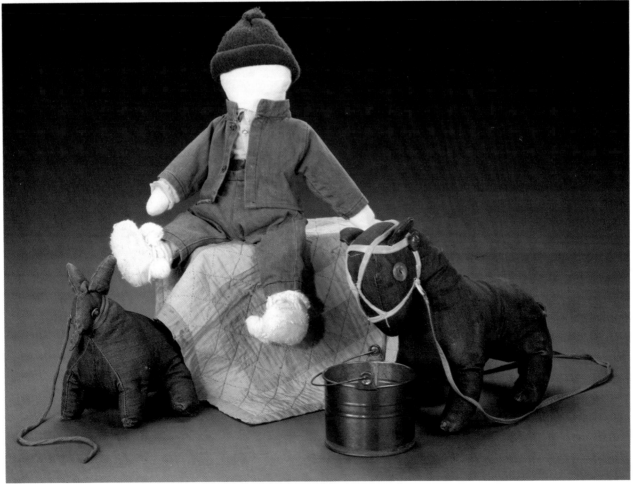

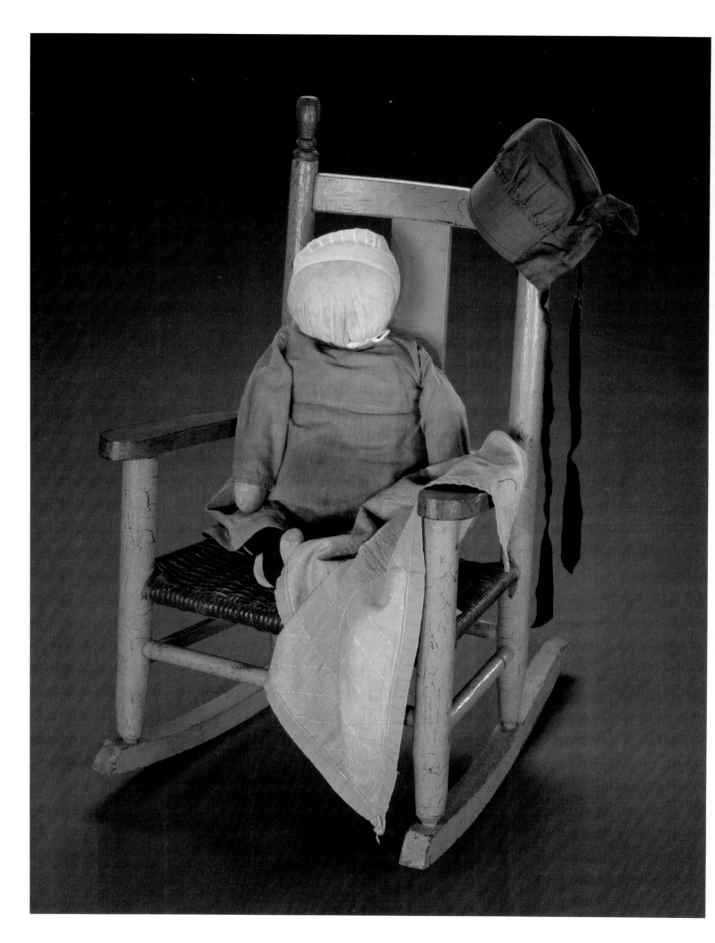

ealistic doll is.

Sometimes mothers have made the animals or dolls. Sometimes an older sister or other relative made the toys, or little girls created them for themselves. "Grandmother made a donkey for me out of flannel material, with a mane and tail," one animal lover recalls.

On a farm, animals are companions for adult and child alike. Tales of children with pet chickens and cats, of rabbits in dresses and dogs in cradles, are common. One person remembers, "We had a black pony, Daisy. There were seven girls and one boy in our family, with the boy about in the middle. Anyway, he was given the pony for Christmas one year, complete with harness and open buggy. I, being the youngest, had many a happy ride in the buggy, and when the cousins would come, we'd give them rides. Whenever company came, they always wanted a ride." If a live pony wasn't available, imagination provided an alternative. Many children played horse with their siblings and cousins. The harness and lines were readily adapted from denim suspenders or baler twine.

Togetherness is important in an Amish child's enjoyment of life, and it is a value the Amish know will not happen automatically. Fostering it demands making conscious decisions. In addition to opting against cars in order to keep the family closer, Amish parents give much time to interaction with their children. Many youngsters remember with joy, riding along with Father as he plowed the fields or mixing up batches of cookies with Mother.

Extended Family Is a Resource

There is a strong intergenerational element in Amish households as well, due to the fact that the Amish care for their own elderly, often building additions onto their farmhouses for the older couples. Skills, stories, and wisdom are thus passed from grandparents to grandchildren.

"Grandma made satchels out of black oilcloth with dark material bound around the edges and closed with overshoe buckles," recalls one happy recipient. "She made and gave them to all her granddaughters for Christmas as they became old enough to enjoy playing with dolls."

Mothers and children have frequently converted mail-order catalogues into pretend families and households. One woman forgot her paper family's name but remembers, "We played with them as long as we could, as catalogues were only gotten by mail once a year." A homemade solution of flour and water served as paste, and empty matchboxes as tables and benches.

Cradle and doll, 1900–1910. Cradle-wood, 8¾ × 15½ × 11½. Doll oil cloth head with sock body. 9½" high. Wayne County, Ohio. Collection of Kathryn and Dan McCauley.

Other children cut pictures of furniture out of the catalogues, drew floor plans, and had a full wardrobe of clothes for their paper figures. Farm magazines provided the necessary cutouts to stock the barns and sheds with animals and implements.

The memories of an Amish woman from Maryland embody many significant characteristics of Amish playthings. "My sister made some sewing cards for me and I sewed them," she said. The cards were likely constructed from cardboard and shoelaces already on hand in the home without need for sophisticated technology. One sibling made the toy for another. There was creativity expended by both designer and sewer. And finally, the toy taught, through play, skills that the child needed later in life.

Lunch Pail, *1950–70. 10½ × 4½ × 8. Lancaster County, Pennsylvania. Collection of Kathryn and Dan McCauley.*

Cat, *1920s. Upholstery fabric, 12½ × 6 × 7½. Lancaster County, Pennsylvania. Ron and Marilyn Kowaleski.*

Rabbit, *1900s. Rayon body, cotton tail, button eyes, 3 × 5 × 2½. Pennsylvania. Stone House Antiques, Phoenix, Arizona.*

Teddy Bear, c. 1940. Wool, 15" high. The People's Place, Intercourse, Pennsylvania.

Teddy Bear, 1920–40. Straw stuffed, 11" high. Lancaster County, Pennsylvania. Collection of Kathryn and Dan McCauley. The dress was made for the teddy bear by an Amish mother when her daughter requested a doll.

Squirrel, *1920s. Upholstery fabric, 5½ × 2½ × 3½. Lancaster County, Pennsylvania. Ron and Marilyn Kowaleski.*

Rabbit, *c. 1910. Cotton, 3½ × 5 × 3¾. Lancaster County, Pennsylvania. I Love Country, Intercourse, Pennsylvania.*

Dog, *1943. Corduroy with rag stuffing, 9 × 7½. Holmes County, Ohio. Collection of Kathryn and Dan McCauley.*

Dog, *c. 1935. Wool, 8 × 10 × 9. Lancaster County, Pennsylvania. I Love Country, Intercourse, Pennsylvania.*

Dog, *1920. Denim body stuffed with cotton rags, 7 × 4½. Holmes County, Ohio. Collection of Eve and David Wheatcroft.*

Mule, *c. 1890. Cotton, 4 × 6 × 3. Lancaster County, Pennsylvania. I Love Country, Intercourse, Pennsylvania.*

Mule, *1900–1910. Cotton stuffed with straw, 10 × 7. Holmes County, Ohio. Collection of Kathryn and Dan McCauley.*

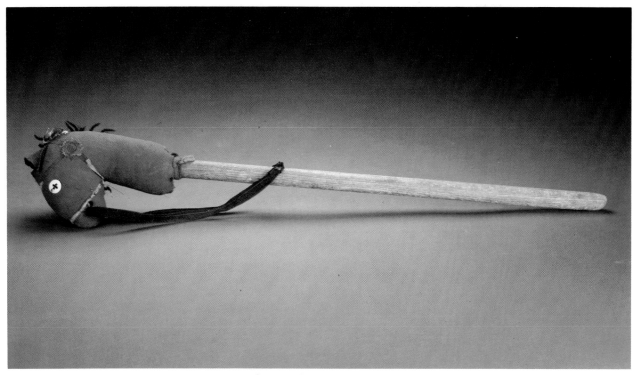

Stick horse, *1930–40. 36″ long. Lancaster County, Pennsylvania. Collection of Kathryn and Dan McCauley.*

Horse, *1910. Denim body stuffed with cotton rags, 10″ tall × 5″ wide. Holmes County, Ohio. Collection of Eve and David Wheatcroft.*

Farm Animals, *1930–40. Hand-painted on wood. Lancaster County, Pennsylvania. Collection of Kathryn and Dan McCauley.*

Ball in Cup Toy, *c. 1890. Wood, 10″ long. Holmes County, Ohio. Collection of Barbara S. Janos, New York, NY.*

Wooden Blocks, *c. 1940. Lancaster County, Pennsylvania. Courtesy of David E. Riehl.*

Horse, *c. 1850. Wood, 10¹⁄₈ × 9¹⁄₂ × 3¹⁄₂. Holmes County, Ohio. Collection of Barbara S. Janos, New York, NY.*

Doll Bed, *c. 1910. Wool, 14 × 8 × 4. Lancaster County,*
Pennsylvania. Courtesy of David E. Riehl.

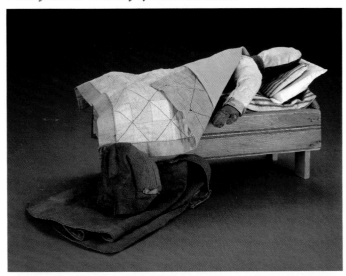

Doll Cradle, *1918. Oak with feather mattress, 18 × 5½.*
Holmes County, Ohio. Collection of Stephanie Reynolds and
Steve Caldwell.

Bed, *1930. Wood with straw tick mattress, 16 × 14 × 20.*
Lancaster County, Pennsylvania. Privately owned.

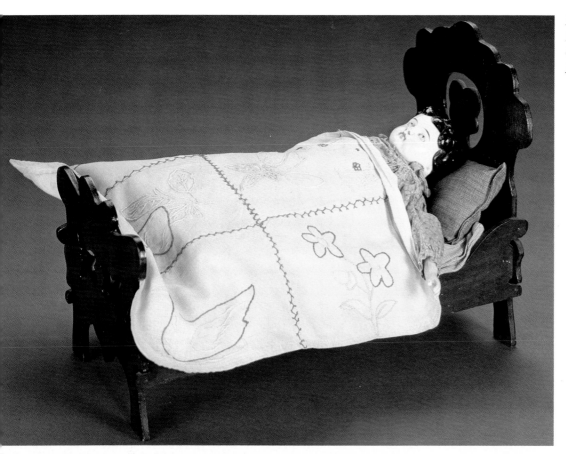

Bed, c. 1930. Pine,
13 × 8 × 10. Lancaster
County, Pennsylvania.
Privately owned.

Miniature Chest,
1870–80. Pine,
10¾ × 15 × 7¼.
Mifflin County,
Pennsylvania.
Collection of Kathryn
and Dan McCauley.

Who Are These People?

The Amish are a Christian group with roots in the 16th-century Protestant Reformation in Europe. At the time of the Reformation, a person became a member of the state (Roman Catholic) church at birth. Numerous people, however, came more and more to question this tenet, as well as other doctrines and the increasingly rampant corruption among church hierarchy, and set out to "reform" the church. The most radical wing of the Reformation felt strongly that a more faithful church would be a "believers' church," with all members equal in the sight of God. It was to God that one owed ultimate allegiance, despite the demands of government. They were furthermore convinced that baptism should only follow a voluntary, adult commitment to Christ and his church. Hence they were nicknamed, Anabaptists, or "re-baptizers."

Following the first adult baptism of three leaders on January 21, 1525, in Switzerland, the Anabaptist movement spread throughout Europe. They continued to add to their number despite severe persecution and slaughter at the hands of Catholics and Protestants alike. One group of Anabaptists were eventually called Mennonites, after Menno Simons, a leader and prolific writer.

In 1693, a Mennonite minister from the Alsace, in France, Jacob Amman, was convinced that the Mennonites were becoming too acculturated and forgetting many of the reasons for originally breaking from the state church. In an effort to preserve the purity of the church, Amman led a movement away from the Mennonites. His followers eventually came to be called Amish, a variation on his name.

Today no Amish remain in Europe. They live instead in communities across the eastern and midwestern United States and in one Canadian province, as a growing alternative to mainstream faith and living.

The Amish believe their commitment to Christ and his teachings should permeate all of life. This has caused them to opt against many of the values important to modern society. Church, the fellowship of their community, and family are among the most important elements in an Amish person's life.

To maintain these values, the Amish have traditionally drawn clear lines. When the Amish believe a certain object or practice is likely to undermine the solidarity of church, family, or fellowship, they generally prohibit it. One example is their basic caution against technology. The Old Order Amish, the strictest of the various groups, do not permit members to use electricity from public utilities, to have radios, televisions or telephones in the home, or to own cars. In the case of the latter, the Amish do not see anything intrinsically wrong with automobiles. However, they have observed many families with cars whose responsibilities and energy are scattered among school, work, church, and civic involvements, and who, as a result, spend little time at home together. The Amish see the car as a detriment to family life.

The Amish position on education is grounded in similar reasoning. Extensive formal education often draws people away from rural communities to urban centers. Learning and wisdom are encouraged within Amish communities, but few Amish receive formal education beyond grade eight.

Other distinctives such as plain dress and the Pennsylvania Dutch (a dialect most closely related to German) language set the Amish apart. Again the reasoning is the same. The Amish seek to draw lines short of temptations that might bring them into acculturation and assimilation with the larger world. Their desire is to be "separated unto God," away from the world.

The Amish have become a curiosity for many people caught in the rush of our highly technological modern world. They are fascinated by the quality and wholeness they discover in the lives of the Amish. The more idealistic may flirt with the possibility of joining the Amish; numerous people, at the very least, assess their own lives in comparison to the world of the Amish. The Amish way is a revolutionary, yet viable, alternative to modern life.

Readings and Sources

About Antique Amish Quilts

Bishop, Robert, and Elizabeth Safanda. *A Gallery of Amish Quilts.* New York: E.P. Dutton and Company, Inc., 1976.

Cory, Pepper. *Quilting Designs From the Amish.* Lafayette, California: C&T Publishing, 1985.

Haders, Phyllis. *Sunshine and Shadow: The Amish and Their Quilts.* New York: Universe Books, 1976.

Horton, Roberta. *Amish Adventure.* Lafayette, California: C&T Publishing, 1983.

Lawson, Suzy. *Amish Inspirations.* Cottage Grove, Oregon: Amity Publications, 1982.

Pellman, Rachel T. *Amish Quilt Patterns.* Intercourse, Pennsylvania: Good Books, 1984.

_____ . *Small Amish Quilt Patterns.* Intercourse, Pennsylvania: Good Books, 1985.

Pellman, Rachel, and Kenneth Pellman. *Amish Crib Quilts.* Intercourse, Pennsylvania: Good Books, 1985.

_____ . *The World of Amish Quilts.* Intercourse, Pennsylvania: Good Books, 1984.

Pottinger, David. *Quilts from the Indiana Amish.* New York: E.P. Dutton, Inc., 1983.

About Other Quilts

Binney, Edward 3rd, and Gail Binney-Winslow. *Homage to Amanda.* San Francisco: RK Press, 1984.

Bonesteel, Georgia. *More Lap Quilting With Georgia Bonesteel.* Birmingham, Alabama: Oxmoor House, Inc., 1985.

Finley, Ruth E. *Old Patchwork Quilts and the Women Who Made Them.* New York: Charles T. Branford Company, 1929.

Fox, Sandi. *Small Endearments: 19th Century Quilts for Children and Dolls.* Los Angeles: The Los Angeles Municipal Art Gallery Associates, 1980.

Haders, Phyllis. *The Warner Collector's Guide to American Quilts.* New York: The Main Street Press, 1981.

Hall, Carrie A., and Rose G. Kretsinger. *The Romance of the Patchwork Quilt in America.* New York: Bonanza Books, 1935.

Holstein, Jonathan. *The Pieced Quilt: An American Design Tradition.* Boston: New York Graphic Society, 1983.

Johnson, Bruce. *A Child's Comfort: Baby and Doll Quilts in American Folk Art.* New York: The Museum of American Folk Art, 1977.

Khin, Yvonne M. *The Collector's Dictionary of Quilt Names and Patterns.* Washington, D.C.: Acropolis Books, Ltd., 1980.

Kiracofe, Roderick, and Michael Kile. *The Quilt Digest.* San Francisco: Kiracofe and Kile, 1983.

_____ . *The Quilt Digest.* San Francisco: Kiracofe and Kile, 1984.

McCloskey, Marsha. *Wall Quilts.* Bothell, Washington: That Patchwork Place, 1983.

Murwin, Susan Aylsworth, and Suzzy Chalfant Payne. *Quick and Easy Patchwork on the Sewing Machine.* New York: Dover Publications, 1979.

Pellman, Rachel T., and Joanne Ranck. *Quilts Among the Plain People.* Intercourse, Pennsylvania: Good Books, 1981.

Soltow, Willow Ann. *Making Animal Quilts: Patterns and Projects.* Intercourse, Pennsylvania: Good Books, 1986.

Tomlonson, Judy Schroeder. *Mennonite Quilts and Pieces.* Intercourse, Pennsylvania: Good Books, 1985.

Woodard, Thos. K., and Blanche Greenstein. *Crib Quilts and Other Small Wonders.* New York: E.P. Dutton, Inc., 1981.

About the Amish

Amish Cooking. Aylmer, Ontario: Pathway Publishing House, 1965.

Bender, H.S. *The Anabaptist Vision.* Scottdale, Pennsylvania: Herald Press, 1967.

Braght, Thieleman J. van, comp. *The Bloody Theatre; or, Martyrs Mirror.* Scottdale, Pennsylvania: Herald Press, 1951.

Budget, The. A weekly newspaper serving the Amish and Mennonite communities. Sugarcreek, Ohio, 1890–.

Family Life. Amish periodical published monthly. Aylmer, Ontario: Pathway Publishing House.

Fisher, Sara E., and Rachel K. Stahl. *The Amish School.* Intercourse, Pennsylvania: Good Books, 1985.

Gingerich, Orland. *The Amish of Canada.* Waterloo, Ontario: Conrad Press, 1972.

Good, Merle. *Who Are the Amish?.* Intercourse, Pennsylvania: Good Books, 1986.

_____ , and Phyllis Pellman Good. *20 Most Asked Questions About the Amish and Mennonites.* Intercourse, Pennsylvania: Good Books, 1979.

Good, Phyllis Pellman, and Rachel Thomas Pellman. *From Amish and Mennonite Kitchens.* Intercourse, Pennsylvania: Good Books, 1984.

Hostetler, John A. *Amish Life.* Scottdale, Pennsylvania: Herald Press, 1959.

_____ . *Amish Society.* Baltimore: Johns Hopkins University Press, 1963.

_____ , and Gertrude E. Huntingdon. *Children in Amish Society.* New York: Holt, Rhinehart and Winston, Inc., 1971.

Keim, Albert N. *Compulsory Education and the Amish.* Boston: Beacon Press, 1975.

Klaassen, Walter. *Anabaptism: Neither Catholic Nor Protestant.* Waterloo, Ontario: Conrad Press, 1982.

Ruth, John L. *A Quiet and Peaceable Life.* Intercourse, Pennsylvania: Good Books, 1985.

Scott, Stephen. *Plain Buggies—Amish, Mennonite and Brethren Horse-Drawn Transportation.* Intercourse, Pennsylvania: Good Books, 1981.

_____ . *Why Do They Dress That Way?.* Intercourse, Pennsylvania: Good Books, 1986.

Index

Amish doll clothing, 43, 44, 46, 47
Amish dolls, antique, (photos), 48–77
Amish dolls (antique), characteristics of, 43, 44, 46
Amish dolls (contemporary), characteristics of, 47
Amish toys (photos), 84–93
Amish toys, characteristics of, 79, 80
Amman, Jacob, 94
Anabaptists, 94
Antique Amish quilts (definition of), 7, 8

BARS, 30, 31
BARS AND BLOCKS, 32
BARS, CONCENTRIC, 33
Bicycles, 80
Bottle doll (photo), 52
BOW TIE, 36, 37

CHECKERBOARD, 20, 21
CHINESE COINS, 32, 33
Color, as a sign of geographic origin of quilts, 8
Color in antique Amish quilts, 7, 8
Color in contemporary Amish quilts, 7, 8
CONCENTRIC BARS, 33
Convictions, 44, 46, 80, 83, 94
Creativity (in the Amish community), 7
Crib quilts, 8

"Distinctives" (of the Amish), 94
Doll quilts (photos), 12-41
Dolls, antique Amish, characteristics of, 43, 44, 46
Dolls, contemporary Amish, characteristics of, 47
Dolls (photos), 48-77
"Drawing lines" (in the Amish community), 7, 43, 94

Education, Amish position on, 94
EMBROIDERED QUILT, 40

Fabric in antique Amish quilts, 7, 8
Fabric in contemporary Amish quilts, 7, 8
Faceless dolls, 43, 44, 47
Family relationships, 83
Family size, 80
Fishing, 80
FLAG STARS, 38
FOUR-PATCH, 20, 22, 24, 25, 27, 28

Geographic locations of Amish communities, 8, 94

JOB'S TEARS, 38

Lancaster County, Pennsylvania, Amish, 8, 44
Lizzie Lapp, 44
Lizzie Lapp dolls, 44
LOG CABIN, 34

Mennonites, 94
Mifflin County, Pennsylvania, Amish, 8

NINE-PATCH, 24, 25, 28

ONE-PATCH, 16, 17, 18, 19, 23
OPEN SQUARE, 30

Patterns, as sign of geographic origin of quilts, 8
Patterns, common antique Amish quilt, 8, 11
Pets, 83
PINWHEEL STAR, 40
PLAIN, 29
Protestant Reformation, 94

Quilting, in antique Amish quilts, 7, 8
Quilting, in contemporary Amish quilts, 7, 8
Quilting, necessity of, 8

Quilts, doll (photos), 12-41

Recreation, 79, 80, 83

Sewing skills (of Amish girls), 7
Sex roles (in the Amish community), 11, 46
SHOO-FLY, 41
Simons, Menno, 94
STARS, 38, 39
Stilts, 80
STREAK OF LIGHTNING, 34, 35
SUNSHINE AND SHADOW, 12, 13, 14, 15
Swartzendruber Amish (Ohio), 43, 44

Teddy bears (photos), 85
Toy furniture (photos), 92, 93
Toys, Amish (photos), 84–93
Toys, Amish, characteristics of, 79, 80
Tricycles, 80
TRIP AROUND THE WORLD, 14
Triplet dolls (photo), 50
Twin dolls (photos), 57, 74, 75

Values (in the Amish community), 83, 95

Work, 7, 8, 11, 79, 80

UPPER CASE = quilt pattern names

About the Authors

The Pellmans are well-known as the authors of THE WORLD OF AMISH QUILTS and AMISH CRIB QUILTS.

Rachel Thomas Pellman is manager of The Old Country Store in Intercourse, Pennsylvania, which features quilts, crafts, and toys made by more than 250 Amish and Mennonite craftspersons. A graduate of Eastern Mennonite College, she has written AMISH QUILT PATTERNS and SMALL AMISH QUILT PATTERNS. She has also co-authored QUILTS AMONG THE PLAIN PEOPLE, FROM AMISH AND MENNONITE KITCHENS, and 12 Pennsylvania Dutch Cookbooks.

Kenneth R. Pellman is manager of The People's Place, an educational center concerned with Amish and Mennonite arts, faith and culture. Kenny graduated from Eastern Mennonite College, where he taught drama for one year. His photography appears in several books, including a National Geographic publication. He is currently working on two more manuscripts that deal with Amish and Mennonite themes.

The Pellmans were married in 1976. They live in Lancaster, Pennsylvania with their two young sons, Nathaniel and Jesse. They are members of Rossmere Mennonite Church.